YOU UNLOCK THIS DOOR WITH THE KEY OF IMAGINATION....

....BEYOND IT IS ANOTHER DIMENSION....

...A DIMENSION OF SOUND....

HACK! COUGH!

....A DIMENSION OF SIGHT....

....A DIMENSION OF MIND....

$E=mc^2$

....YOU'RE MOVING INTO A LAND OF BOTH SHADOW AND SUBSTANCE....OF THINGS AND IDEAS....

2/27

YOU HAVE JUST CROSSED OVER INTO.....

THE KUDZU ZONE

MAMA, WHERE'S MY OTHER SOCK?

TEE-DEE TEE-DEE, TEE-DEE, TEE-DEE

A DOUBLEWIDE WITH A VIEW

THE KUDZU CHRONICLES

DOUG MARLETTE

LONGSTREET PRESS
Atlanta, Georgia

Published by
LONGSTREET PRESS, INC.
2150 Newmarket Parkway
Suite 102
Marietta, Georgia 30067

Kudzu is syndicated by Creators Syndicate, Los Angeles,
California

Printed in the United States of America

1st printing, 1989

Library of Congress Catalog Number 89-084529

ISBN 0-929264-61-4

This book was printed by Malloy Lithographing Inc., Ann
Arbor, Michigan. Cover design by Jack Sherman.

CONTENTS

For Melinda and Jackson

BYE-BYE, BYPASS

2

3

6

8

9

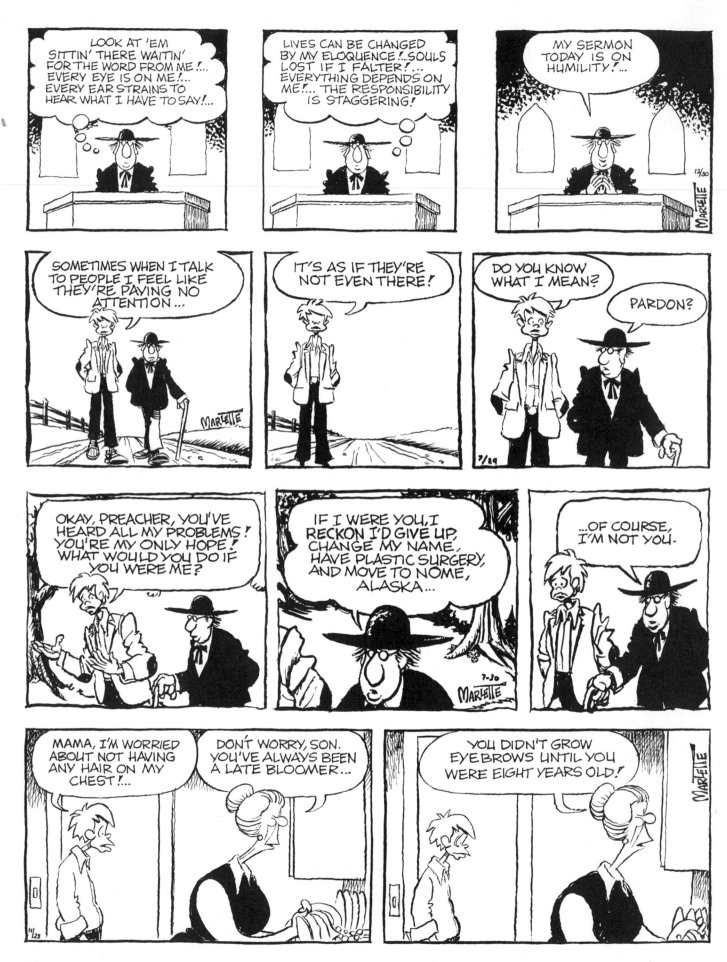

10

14

THE WAR ON PUBERTY

20

21

24

27

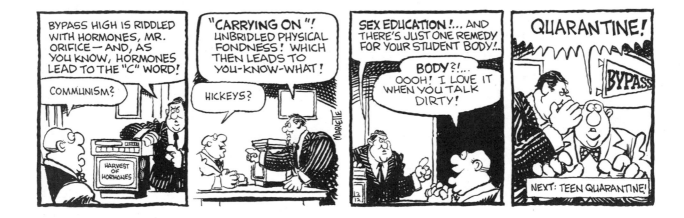

36

LOVE IS BLIND

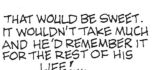

48

49

57

58

60

AMEN, PREACHER

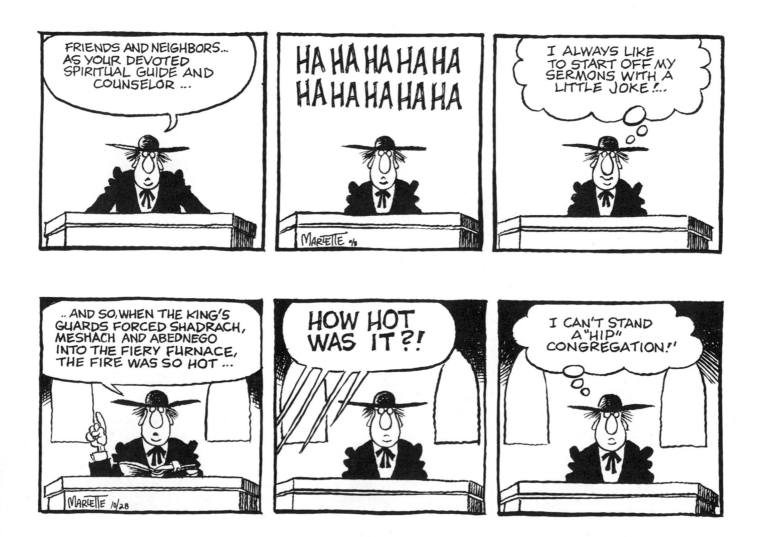

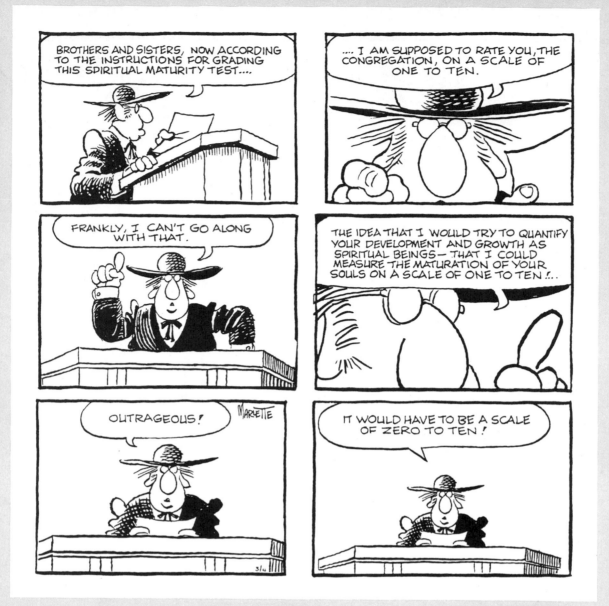

67

68

69

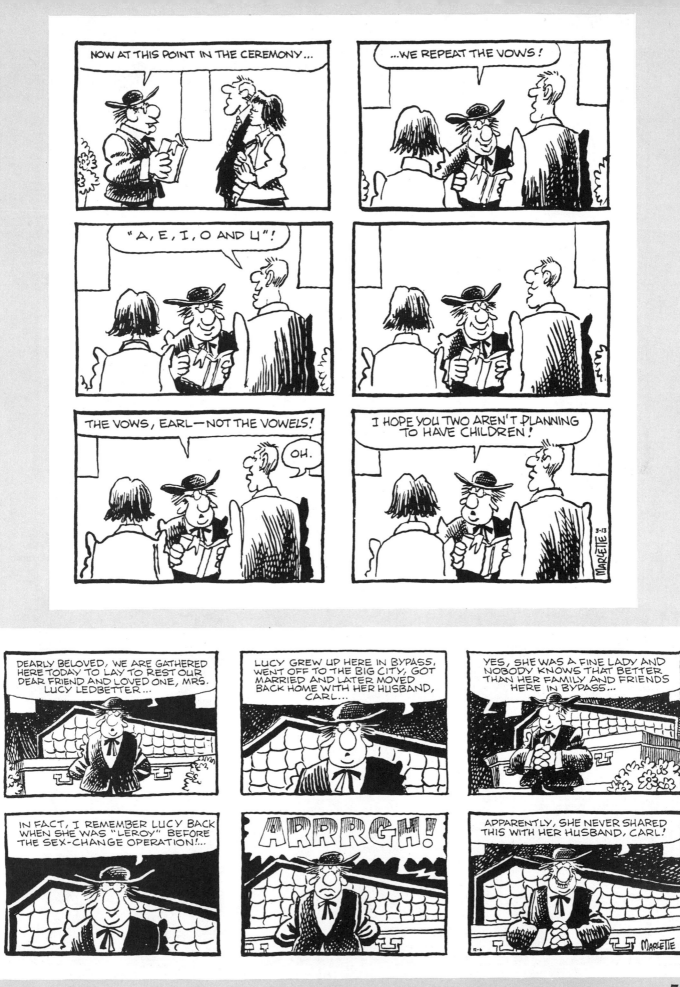

79

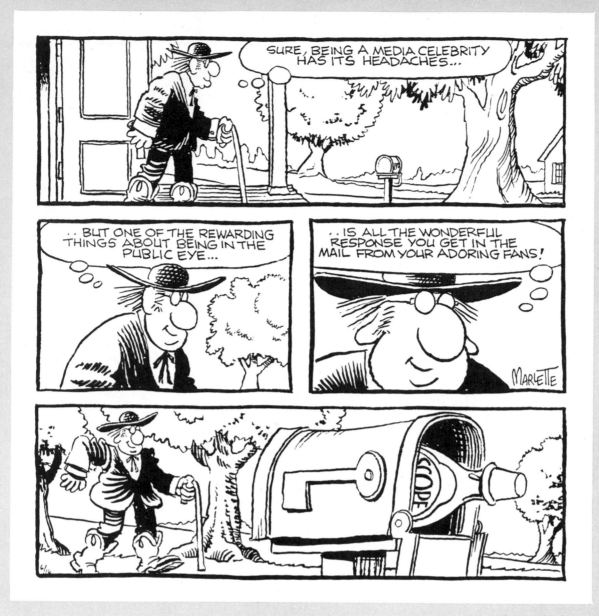

A BIRD IN THE HAND

AAH!...SOMETIMES I LIKE TO THINK BACK TO THE GOOD OLD DAYS IN THE PET SHOP!...

I WAS THE ONLY PARAKEET IN A STORE FULL OF CUTE, CUDDLY, FUZZY LITTLE PUPPIES!...

≷ SIGH ≶

OF COURSE, THE SMELL WOULD NAIL A BUZZARD IN A SEWAGE TREATMENT PLANT!

MARLETTE 2/4

BEING THE ONLY PARAKEET IN A PET SHOP FULL OF PUPPIES WASN'T EASY!...

pets

CUSTOMERS CAME IN AND "OOOHED" AND "AAAHED" OVER THE PUPPIES AND IGNORED ME!...AT THE TIME IT REALLY HURT MY FEELINGS!...

OOOOH!

AAAAH!

IT WASN'T THE PUPS' FAULT BUT I STILL HAD TO FIND A WAY TO DEAL WITH MY JEALOUSY!...

..SO AT NIGHT I'D MOLT IN THEIR GRAVY TRAIN!

MARLETTE

2/5

BUBBACIDE

99

What Exactly IS A 'Good Ol' Boy'?

Is he defined merely by his distinctive tribal trappings?

- CAT HAT
- CHAW
- BIB OVERALLS
- BLUE RIBBON BEER
- BLUE RIBBON BEER GUT
- COON DOG
- PICK-UP TRUCK
- GUN RACK
- MUD FLAPS

WEBSTER'S

MARLETTE 1/10

...OR IS IT THE WAY HE SPITS TOBACCO JUICE?

PTOO!

...OR STRADDLES A CHAIR TO SIT DOWN?..

...OR IS THE WHOLE GREATER THAN THE SUM OF ITS PARTS?

2 + 2 = 5

WE AT THIS COMIC STRIP BELIEVE "GOOD OL' BOYNESS" IS NOT JUST AN ATTITUDE, A GESTURE, OR AN UNINTELLIGIBLE ACCENT... IT'S A WAY OF LIFE!

ON THE VERGE OF EXTINCTION!

DISTINGUISHED PANEL OF EXPERTS

THE RISE

MANY CULTURAL ANTHROPOLOGISTS CONSIDER THE DECADE 1975-1985 AS THE "GOLDEN AGE OF THE GOOD OL' BOY"

COUNTRY MUSIC EXPANDED ITS AUDIENCE...

♪ OLD FLAMES CAIN'T HOLD A CANDLE TO YOU... ♪

THEY'RE PLAYING OUR SONG!

...THE C.B. CRAZE HIT

TEN-FOUR, GOOD BUDDY!

JOHN TRAVOLTA'S FILM HOMAGE "URBAN COWBOY" USHERED IN "REDNECK CHIC"...

PUTTIN' ON TH' GRITZ!

MARLETTE

A ROLE MODEL "FIRST BROTHER" EVEN SHOWED UP IN THE WHITE HOUSE...

...BUT SOON THE BUCKING MACHINES WOULD STAND RIDERLESS...

...AS THE EIGHTIES SETTLED IN, "VANITY PLATES" REPLACED C.B. HANDLES

JIMBO

...AND EVEN IN BYPASS, FOLKS FACED THE INEVITABLE...

CAT HATS AND BLOW DRYERS DON'T MIX!

2/5

NEXT: THE FALL!

THE DECLINE OF THE GOOD OL' BOY

SOME HISTORIANS CLAIM THE DEATH KNELL SOUNDED WHEN TEXAS SENT A PREPPIE TO THE U.S. CONGRESS...

JEEPERS, ER...Y'ALL!

BUSH

OTHERS INSIST TAMMY WYNETTE'S REFUSAL TO "STAND BY HER MAN" WAS THE TURNING POINT...

I WANNA D-I-V-O-R-C-E!

STILL OTHERS SAY IT WAS ALL OVER WHEN BILLY CARTER GOT MIXED UP WITH THE LIBYANS!..

MOOLAH BE PRAISED!

...OR WHEN ELVIS BIT THE DUST!..

...AND WHEN WILLIE NELSON SANG A DUET WITH WAYNE NEWTON!... ...WELL...

♪ DANKE SHOEN OOO DANKE SHOEN ♪

MARLETTE

...BUT BYPASS STUNNED A NATION WHEN "MY DINNER WITH ANDRE" OUTDREW "SMOKEY AND THE BANDIT, IX" AT THE STARLITE DRIVE-IN THEATER...

SOMETHIN'S WRONG, MAYBELLE—BAD WRONG!

SNACK BAR

True Life TALES OF VANISHING BUBBAS

MY RAY BOB WAS BORN 'N' BRED A GOOD OL' BOY!...

EXPLAINS MRS. JUANITA RATCHETT

"...THEN ONE FRIDAY NIGHT DURING CHAMPIONSHIP WRASSLIN' HE UP 'N' SEZ:"

BRING ME A PERRIER, JUANITA!

"'COURSE, I IGNORED IT 'TIL THE NEXT DAY HE SEZ:"

LET'S GO ANTIQUEIN', JUANITA!

MARLETTE 9-22

"NEXT THING YA KNOW IT'S:"

TURN DOWN THEM SOAPS, WOMAN—I'M LISSENIN' TA NATIONAL PUBLIC RADIO!

"I KNEW SUMP'N WAS SHO'NUFF WRONG WHEN I WAS PREGNANT WITH OUR SIXTH YOUNG'UN, DEBBIE EARL, AN' HE SEZ:"

JUANITA, HONEY, THIS TIME LET'S DO LAMAZE!

"BUT I KNOWED I'D LOST HIM FOREVER WHEN HE FED ME A PASTA DISH HE MADE HISSELF!..."

BON APPETIT, SUGAR BOOGER!

RAY BOB RATCHETT— YET ANOTHER VICTIM OF BUBBACIDE!

A RIGHT TO SING
THE BLUES

Y'KNOW, MY MAMA'S BEEN WORKIN' FOR THE TADSWORTH FAMILY FOR AS LONG AS I CAN REMEMBER.

BOY, IS SHE LUCKY!...

MARLETTE   12/6

LUCKY?

YEAH, IMAGINE! SHE PROBABLY KNOWS VERANDA BETTER THAN ANYBODY!

MAZEE!... BRING ME A TOOTHPICK!

I DECLARE, MAZEE, YOU'VE BEEN WITH OUR FAMILY FOR AGES! WHY, YOU PRACTICALLY RAISED ME BY YOURSELF!

LAWD, MISS VERANDA, DON'T GO GIVIN' ME CREDIT I DON'T DESERVE!

I DONE MY BEST, THAT'S TRUE, BUT YOU PRETTY MUCH BEEN LIKE Y'SELF FROM DAY ONE!...

MARLETTE   12/7

WELL, THANK YOU, MAZEE!... I GUESS I DON'T GIVE MYSELF ENOUGH CREDIT!

LAWD KNOWS, GIRL, YOU DESERVE IT!

108

113

116

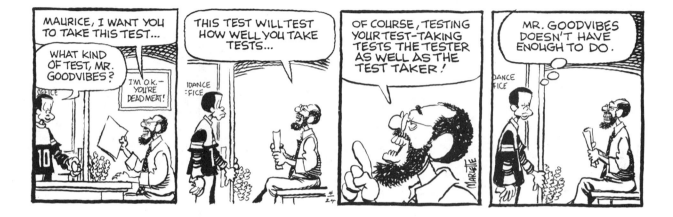

GIMME THAT
PRIME TIME RELIGION

122

134

135

142

"THE SHRINE OF BYPASS" HITS THE TABLOIDS:

IRRATIONAL ENQUIRER
ELVIS SNEERS FROM BEYOND THE GRAVE
LIZ WEDS UFO ALIEN

CELEBRITIES STEP FORWARD TO VOUCH FOR THE SHRINE'S AUTHENTICITY...

I RAN INTO ELVIS ON THE ASTRAL PLANE AND HE SAYS IT'S HIM ALL RIGHT!

THANK YOU, MISS MACLAINE.

AN AD HOC COMMITTEE OF NOBEL LAUREATES DEBUNK IT AS SUPERSTITIOUS NONSENSE:

HORSE FEATHERS!

CA-CA-!

HOG WASH!

NOTED SECULAR HUMANISTS AGREE:

STUDIES SHOW IT'S ALL DUE TO LACK OF SELF-ESTEEM!

MR. GOODVIBES

...YET SOME DOCTORS OF MEDICINE TURN TO THE "MIRACLE OF THE BLACK VELVET ELVIS" AS A LAST RESORT!...

TAKE TWO ASPIRIN, VISIT "THE SHRINE OF BYPASS" AND CALL ME IN THE MORNING!

NOTED SECULAR HUMANIST NATHAN GOODVIBES INVESTIGATES THE SUPERNATURAL CLAIMS OF THE "SHRINE OF BYPASS"...

POPPYCOCK!

CAMOUFLAGE!

THE GIG IS UP, PREACHER! I'M EXPOSING YOUR LITTLE SCAM IN THE NEXT ISSUE OF "PSYCHOLOGY TODAY"!

LOOK! ELVIS CURLED HIS LIP AT YOU!.. OH, DARN—YOU MISSED THE MIRACLE AGAIN!

THE GOODVIBES PROBE IS PUBLISHED—A DEVASTATING EXPOSÉ, FULL OF UNDENIABLE FACTS, IRREFUTABLE LOGIC AND THOUGHTFUL ANALYSIS!...THE NEW YORK TIMES REPRINTS IT ALONG WITH AN EDITORIAL CONDEMNING RELIGIOUS CHARLATANS...

ATTENDANCE AT THE "SHRINE OF BYPASS" SKYROCKETS!...

THANK GOD FOR SECULAR HUMANISTS!

ELVIS SHRINE TEESHIRTS

MIRACLE MUGS

NEWS SPREADS OF THE MIRACULOUS CURE WROUGHT BY THE PREACHER'S BLACK VELVET PORTRAIT OF ELVIS...

NASAL'S FACE CLEARED UP!

NO!

PILGRIMS POUR INTO BYPASS HOPING TO CATCH A GLIMPSE OF THE LEGENDARY ROCKER'S HEALING COUNTENANCE...

WHICH WAY TO ELVIS?

NASAL CONDUCTS GUIDED TOURS

...AND I WAS DUSTING ELVIS RIGHT HERE WHEN HE CURLED HIS LIP AT ME!

OOOH...

DOES IT WEEP, TOO?

RIP OFF!

HIS EYES FOLLOW YOU AROUND THE ROOM!

AT FIRST SKEPTICAL, REV. WILL B. DUNN GRADUALLY ACCEPTS HIS STEWARDSHIP ROLE AS CUSTODIAN OF THIS MODERN-DAY WONDER...

GET YOUR MIRACLE MUGS AND SOUVENIR FLY-SWATTERS!

TEE-SHI

TRUE LIFE TESTIMONIES
TO THE "MIRACLE OF THE BLACK VELVET ELVIS"...

WHEN I LAID EYES ON IT MY FACE CLEARED UP!

MINE BROKE OUT!

MY BACK HASN'T ACTED UP SINCE ELVIS CURLED HIS LIP AT ME!

I HAVEN'T TOUCHED AN "M & M" SINCE!

THE EXPIRATION DATE ON MY MASTERCARD DISAPPEARED!

THE SHRINE OF BYPASS WORKED WONDERS FOR MY RATINGS!

143

THE JOY OF WIMPINESS

147

152

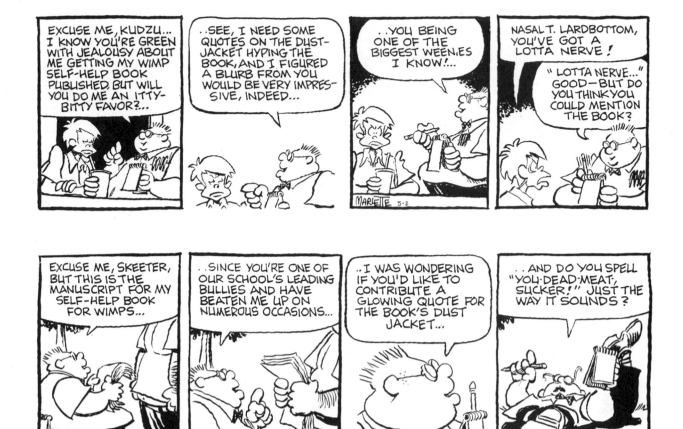

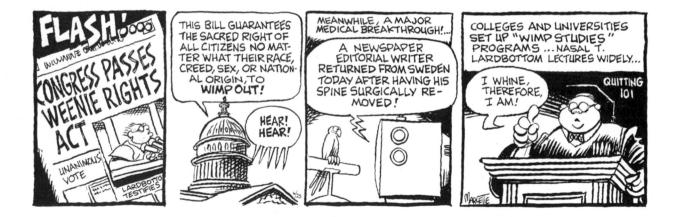

155

CHOCOLATE DREAMS

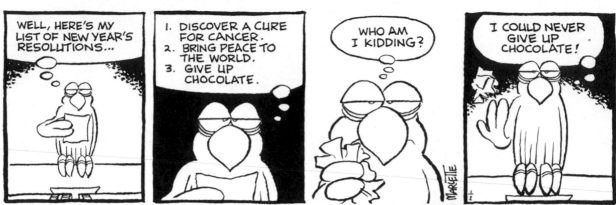

163

164

AIR NASAL

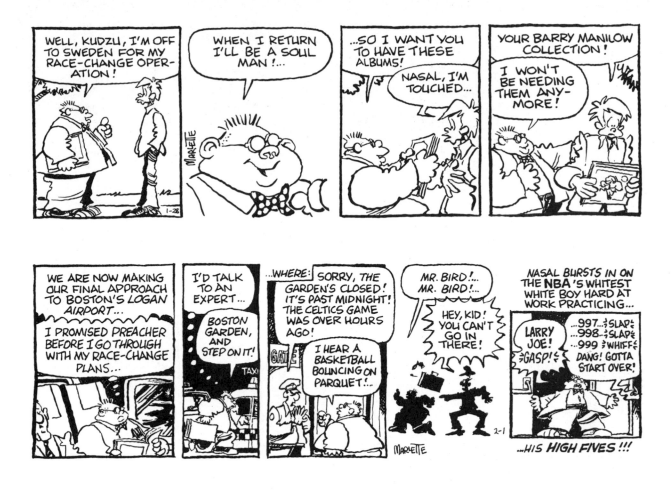

EVEN BEFORE HIS RACE-LIFT BANDAGES COME OFF NASAL BASKS IN HIS NEW-FOUND ATTITUDE !...

APPEARING IN A SPOTLIGHT DANCE ON "SOULTRAIN"...

...REJOINING WILL B. DUNN'S PRESIDENTIAL CAMPAIGN AS OFFICIAL MINORITY LIAISON, HIS ORATORY ELECTRIFIES !...

WILLPOWER, NOT KILLPOWER! FROM THE STEEPLE TO THE PEOPLE!... FROM THE JAM BOX TO THE BALLOT BOX!

HE DOES PUBLIC SERVICE SPOTS FOR THE "WHITE MAN'S DISEASE" FOUNDATION...

THE SLOW !... THE WHITE! THE FLAT-FOOTED! WON'T YOU HELP?

... AND EVEN DREAMS OF DESIGNING HIS OWN SNEAKERS FOR NIKE ...

AIR NASAL

WHEN DO THE RACE-LIFT BANDAGES COME OFF, NASAL?

TONIGHT AT THE SLAM DUNK AND HANG-TIME CONTESTS!

THAT EVENING NASAL SLAMS AND JAMS HIS WAY TO VICTORY...

THEN ANNOUNCES:

LADIES AND GENTLEMEN, BEFORE THE HANG-TIME COMPETITION FINALE, I WANT TO SHED THIS LAST VESTIGE OF MY PAST AS THE WHITEST WHITE BOY AT BYPASS HIGH...

...AND CONCLUDE THE DAY AS THE GENUINE, AUTHENTIC, FULL-FLEDGED BROTHER I WAS DESTINED TO BE: NASAL TYRONE LARDBOTTOM!

NASAL REMOVES HIS RACE-CHANGE SURGERY BANDAGES AS ALL OF BYPASS LOOKS ON...

...THE ARMORY CROWD FALLS SILENT IN ANTICIPATION AS NASAL'S GAUZE IS REMOVED...

...A GASP OF STUNNED DISBELIEF ERUPTS FROM THE ONLOOKERS AS THE HANDIWORK OF THE SWEDISH SURGEON'S SCALPEL IS REVEALED...

¡GASP!¿

WHAT TH-?

HOLY CATFISH!

...FOR BEFORE THEM STILL STANDS THE WHITEST WHITE BOY AT BYPASS HIGH...

...UNAWARES!

NASAL HAS REMOVED HIS RACE-LIFT BANDAGES TO REVEAL HE REMAINS, TO THE ASTONISHMENT OF ALL, THE WHITEST WHITE BOY AT BYPASS HIGH...

THE CROWD IS SLACK-JAWED AS NASAL WARMS UP FOR HIS HANG-TIME COMPETITION, UNAWARE HE IS STILL A CAUCASIAN...

BOINGA! BOINGA! BOING!

THE OPERATION DIDN'T TAKE!

IT WAS PHONY!

IT'S A RIP-OFF!

NASAL'S A COUNTERFEIT BROTHER!

...THEY WHISPER !...

...BUT EVERYONE IN BYPASS IS JUST TOO DARN POLITE TO BRING IT UP.

IN YO' FACE, SUCKER!

THE FOLLOWING YEAR ...

NASAL T. LARDBOTTOM IS AN ASPIRING *BROTHER*:

HE IS FLUENT IN *JIVE*:

YO MAMA! WHAT IT BE! I AIN'T PLAYIN' WITCHA!

HE CAN *HIGH-FIVE* WITHOUT INJURING HIMSELF ... (OR OTHERS.)

MY MAN!

HE HAS MASTERED INTRICATE GREETINGS AND HAND-SHAKES...

HE HAS WORN *DASHIKIS* TO SCHOOL

WE BAD!

...AND HE EVEN UNDERWENT AN UNSUCCESSFUL RACE-CHANGE OPERATION AND SOUL IMPLANT PROCEDURE...

PHOOEY!

...BUT HOW IS HIS AMBITION AND DRIVE REWARDED?

NASAL T. LARDBOTTOM

WHITEST WHITE BOY

5-23 STAY TUNED...

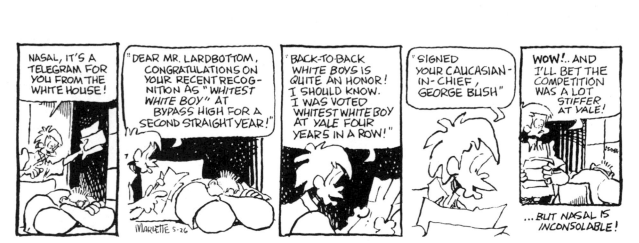

DISTRAUGHT OVER BEING PICKED "WHITEST WHITE BOY" AT BYPASS HIGH YET AGAIN, NASAL REPAIRS TO THE SOLI- TUDE OF HIS ROOM TO CONTEMPLATE THE CRUELTY OF HIS FATE.

NASAL, COME OUT!

NO!

NASAL, IT'S NOT THE END OF THE WORLD — YOUR FRIENDS STILL CARE EVEN IF YOU ARE A WHITE BOY!

YOU'RE NOT THE ONLY GUY WITH ZERO VERTICAL LEAP!

...BUT NASAL BROODS OVER THE ABSURDITY OF EXISTENCE:

DO I REALLY WANT TO LIVE IN A WORLD WHERE THEY CAN JAIL JAMES BROWN...?

...AND BESTOW BACK-TO-BACK "WHITE BOYS" ON A RIGHTEOUS DUDE LIKE ME?

NASAL, IT'S A TELEGRAM FOR YOU FROM THE WHITE HOUSE!

"DEAR MR. LARDBOTTOM, CONGRATULATIONS ON YOUR RECENT RECOG- NITION AS "WHITEST WHITE BOY" AT BYPASS HIGH FOR A SECOND STRAIGHT YEAR!"

"BACK-TO-BACK WHITE BOYS IS QUITE AN HONOR! I SHOULD KNOW. I WAS VOTED WHITEST WHITE BOY AT YALE FOUR YEARS IN A ROW!"

"SIGNED YOUR CAUCASIAN- IN-CHIEF, GEORGE BUSH"

WOW!.. AND I'LL BET THE COMPETITION WAS A LOT STIFFER AT YALE!

...BUT NASAL IS INCONSOLABLE!

VOTED "WHITEST WHITE BOY" AT BYPASS HIGH FOR AN UNPRE- CEDENTED SECOND STRAIGHT YEAR NASAL DOES WHAT ANY RED- BLOODED AMERI- CAN DOES WHEN TRAGEDY STRIKES: HE HITS THE TALK SHOWS!

BACK-TO-BACK "WHITE BOYS"! NASAL, TELL US— HOW DID YOU DO IT?

I DON'T UNDERSTAND, PREACHER — I SPEAK JIVE FLUENTLY!...I MEMORIZED ALL THE MOTOWN LYRICS!...

I ZEROXED MY HAND, TAPED IT TO THE WALL, AND POUNDED MY FINGERS TO A BLOODY PULP PRACTICING MY *HIGH FIVES*!

THAT'S A *WHITE BOY* ALL RIGHT!

Doug Marlette was born in Greensboro, North Carolina, and grew up in Durham, North Carolina, Laurel, Mississippi, and Sanford, Florida.

Both his editorial cartoons and his comic strip *Kudzu* are syndicated in hundreds of newspapers worldwide. He has won every major award for editorial cartooning, including the 1988 Pulitzer Prize. He is the only cartoonist to have received the prestigious Nieman Fellowship at Harvard University.

He spent fifteen years at the *Charlotte Observer*, two years at the *Atlanta Constitution* and now draws editorial cartoons for *New York Newsday*. His work is reprinted regularly in *Newsweek*, the *New York Times* and the *Washington Post*, and he is occasionally featured on "CBS Morning News," "Good Morning, America," ABC's "Nightline" and National Public Radio's "Morning Edition."

Marlette lectures widely at universities, seminaries and divinity schools. His *Kudzu* character Reverend Will B. Dunn, a favorite nationally with clergy of all denominations, is often quoted in sermons and reprinted in church bulletins and the pages of the *Christian Century*.

He co-wrote with novelist Pat Conroy the screenplay "EX," soon to be a feature film from Sandollar Productions.

Marlette lives with his wife, Melinda, and son, Jackson, on the Upper West Side of Manhattan.